The Trump House

David Klein

For Dawne Estep

CONTENTS

The Trump House begins with a dream:

Donald Trump walks onto the stage, the sky is blue, people are all over. We are somewhere in the middle of Ohio, it's the biggest political rally in history, as if the entire United States population arrived, spread across the vast farmland. The corn and wheat has been harvested and the fields are undulating with red caps and t-shirts and signs, "Trump! Trump!"

President-Elect Trump speaks into the microphone, "Citizens of the United States! God Bless you! Thank you for coming today! Thank you for your vote!

Trump is swelling and rising into the sky. Many American's have been waiting years for a moment like this, to have someone they truly believe will benefit the country as their leader. The crowd swells, the sun burns brighter and the landscape is ablaze with red and gold.

Trump declares, "We will make America great again!" The crowd boils to a joyful hysteria. "And, folks, I have two words I must share with our current leaders! Are you ready!"

The entire world shouts, "Yes!"

Trump says, in a low powerful voice, "President Obama!" There's a pause as the red caps begin to fly into the sky, "You're fired!"

Wake up, and Donald Trump, however, has handled his President-Elect of the United States with humility and kinship, "It is time for us to come together as one united people," he declared on election night. "I pledge to every citizen of our land, that I will be a president for all Americans."

He displayed equal brotherhood when he visited with President Obama at the White House on November 10, 2016. During the visit, Trump understood the gravity of what was happening and saw his duty to the country no longer from a distance or as an outsider, but that he will be responsible for the nation. You could see it on his face as he toured the White House.

Donald has evolved into a leader - the composition of his family, his media pursuits, business dealings, and relationships worldwide. Yet, many people are in disbelief that he won, and have not allowed a plausible reason for this reality.

"How did this happen!" Many Hillary supporters were devastated. Tears streamed down the faces of young men and women at the Hillary HQ in New York, as the votes tallied for Trump.

In hundreds of YouTube videos, Hillary supporters vented their anguish. One girl screamed for an ambulance, "I cannot believe this is happening! This has to be a joke! I can't believe this is happening... I'm literally going to die, I need an ambulance!"

These are real reactions. Real feelings. The disbelief flowed through many overlapping groups: those who didn't support Trump, those who hated Trump through their own senses, the uninformed Hillary voter, the informed Hillary voter, and a vast majority of the media.

One CNN reporter exclaimed, "People have talked about a miracle. I'm hearing about a nightmare. It's hard to be a parent tonight... How will I explain this to my children?"

Many republicans were also surprised that Trump won, even though they are pleased with the outcome, and Trump also have questions too, despite the win.

So who is this book for? Why did Trump win? How was The Trump House built? The events that unfolded up to the 2016 election were unprecedented in American history. So it's not an easy answer. But I've laid out the important facts and particular events in a linear way, which speak to the reasons why both candidates won and lost votes. I've watched so much media in the past 15 months that I've turned into a TV set myself. I've scoured books, interviews, the internet, and all the major news programs as much as I could, in real time, and as research. More than a full-time job.

This book is for everyone, although, I get a particular inspiration to write when I see the reactions of Hillary supporters who are honestly at a loss. This is book is truly for them. I genuinely hope they can someday understand why people love Trump.

The Trump House was written also for the Trump supporter who wants to maintain in his mind the events that led to Trump's win. Or to relive it. But it's not enough for the Trump victor to say, "I know why he won, he's awesome!" Then match a personal reason to Trump's agenda, such as taxes or more jobs. Trump's agenda was crucial to voters, but Trump's success at the polls goes deeper than that.

The book is for the Ted Cruz supporter and the Bernie Sanders supporter. It is for voters who were on the fence, and for the types of people ranging from fanatics obsessed with the 2016 Presidential Election (like me) to those who are only mildly interested and ask, "Hey, what was that all about?"

I cover it all. I've enjoyed putting this together and I hope you enjoy reading The Trump House, and even look upon it as a reference for years to come.

So let's get busy, and go to the first brick right now.

THE FIRST BRICK

It's not the media attention and Trump trappings from "The Apprentice" that built the first brick in The Trump House. Of course, we can say that the first brick is Trump's birth in 1946, or when his father was born. Or when the Office of the President of the United States was created, 1789.

Perhaps we can point to any moment when young Trump attended the New York Military Academy, where he was promoted to Captain in his senior year, then again in the same year into the administration building. The *administration building*. That's a good one, right?

Maybe it was a scrape with another kid where he grew up in Jamaica Estates, NY that gave us the Donald we know. Or we can point to his string of successes and failures in real estate and gaming all over the world. We can point to his flirtations with running for president in the 1980's where in 1987 he ran a full-page ad in major newspapers criticizing U.S. foreign policy, "There's nothing wrong with America's Foreign Defense Policy that a little backbone can't cure." That was the headline.

Wait! None of these will do. Obviously we should set the first brick in The Trump House as

Trump's official announcement to run for president. He and his wife Melania famously descended the escalator at Trump Tower on June 16, 2015 and made the announcement to a capacity crowd of thousands. Right away, Donald, albeit with notes, began with a seemingly odd stream of consciousness that would become a motif for his campaign, (subdued only slightly by the intervention of the teleprompter nearly a year later into the campaign).

Trump asserted, "I can tell you, some of the candidates, they went in, they didn't know the air conditioner didn't work. They sweated like dogs, they didn't know the room was too big, because they didn't have anybody there. How are they going to beat ISIS?"

The audience response was minimal when Trump paused, no one really understood the connection. It's undoubtedly odd to leap from air conditioners to ISIS in the same few sentences. But here's the reality: Donald doesn't think or express himself like anyone we know about in the political landscape. The point he was making is that our leaders at the time and potential leaders are unprepared to lead. "Our country is in serious trouble," Trump continued, "We don't have victories any more."

Was this June 16th escalator speech the first brick in The Trump House? No. It is a brick for sure, but not the first brick. Ladies and gentleman, we begin really, when it really mattered, on the Oprah Winfrey show! Indeed, we must go back years. Let's start our story in 1988 when Trump is 42 years old, where, when I watch this interview with Trump, I am riveted every time I watch it, and so was Oprah's audience.

This interview with Donald is so significant in the credibility of the now President-Elect Donald Trump, and it's severely under reported in today's media, that I am going to place the meat and potatoes of it right here:

Oprah: "What would you do differently Donald?"

Trump: "I'd make our allies, forgetting about the enemies, you can't talk to them so easily. I'd make our allies pay their fair share. We're a debtor nation. Something is going to happen over next number of years in this country, because you can't keep on losing $200B and yet we let Japan come in and dump everything right into our markets, it's not free trade. If you ever go to Japan right now and sell something, forget about it Oprah, forget about it. They don't have laws against it, they just make it impossible. They come over here and sell their cars, their VCRs, they knock the hell out of our companies. (Reminder: This is 28 years ago.)

And hey, I have tremendous respect for the Japanese people. I mean you can respect somebody that's beating the hell out of you. They are beating the hell out of this country. Kuwait, they live like kings. The poorest person in Kuwait, they live like kings. And yet, they're not paying. We make it possible for them to sell their oil. Why aren't they paying us 25% of what they are making? It's a joke."

Oprah: "This sounds like presidential talk. Would you ever run?"

Trump: "Probably not. But I do get tired of seeing the country ripped off."

Oprah: "Why would you not?"

Trump: "I just don't think I really have the inclination to do it. I love what I am doing, I really like it."

Oprah: "Also doesn't pay as well."

Trump: "But you know, I just probably wouldn't do it Oprah. I probably wouldn't. But I do get tired of seeing what's happening with this country. And if it got so bad, I would never want to rule it out totally because I really am tired of what's happening with this country, how we are really making other people live like kings and we're not."

They talk about the current presidential race, then...

Oprah: "You said though, that if you did run for president, you'd believe you'd win."

Trump: "Well I don't know. I think I'd win. I tell you what, I wouldn't go in to lose. I've never gone in to lose in my life. And if I did decide to do it, I would say that I would have a hell of a chance of winning. Because I think people, I don't know how your audience feels, but I think people are tired of seeing the United States ripped off. And I can't promise you everything, but I can tell you one thing, this country would make one hell of a lot money from those people that for 25 years have taken advantage. It wouldn't be the way it has been. Believe me."

This interview occurred 28 years ago and is one of the first passionate and thoughtful sides of "The Donald" who cares about The United States of America. We can give anchor to this moment for

Trump's seriousness to run for president because the concern and intelligence displayed by Trump in the interview is so obvious, that it should have eclipsed what the established political powers and their media arms tried to truncate, then and now. If there were any politicians in office in 1987 who cared about America's success, they should have embraced Donald Trump right away.

Trump echoed the same sentiment to Rona Barrett in a 1980 interview, talking about being a public servant, "It's a very mean life... but I *would* dedicate my life to this country. But I see it as a mean life, and I also see it as somebody with strong views, and somebody with the kind of views, views that may be a little unpopular, which may be right, but may be unpopular, wouldn't necessarily have a chance at getting elected against somebody with no great brain but a big smile."

This was a quiet interview when Donald was very young, he was very humble, but you can see that his mind was right for the American values landscape. The Trump House began construction in the 1980s, most specifically on the Oprah Winfrey show in 1987, when Americans across the country took note of Trump's straight talk and specific examples of how the U.S. was doing so poorly. You can see the grit and interest in Trump in the faces of the audience. It was Oprah's first year with her own show and viewership was already breaking records. Indeed, Oprah later became the highest-rated talk show in American history.

As for Donald Trump, this was the first brick in The Trump House. It was the beginning of a political curve that would be trending up for years and culminate, literally on election night, into a massive tail straight up into the air, Enterprise Value being fully recognized, and the American voter had spoken.

THEY'RE RAPISTS

What? What did he say?

"Trump is a racist," said Angel, a kid sitting across from me at the poker table, October 2015. "He hates Mexicans. He called my people rapists. I can't vote for him." Then he said jokingly, "He might send me back."

This put the poker players high in their chairs. Everyone was listening now. This was in Pennsylvania too, a crucial state.

"Angel," I said, "Can you vote?"

Sheepishly, he put his arm out and dropped chips into the pot, "No, not really. Lot's of my family does, but I can't."

I let the conversation sit there for a moment, you don't want to get to pushy at a poker table. I liked him too, I had known him for about three years, at least in a poker room kind of way.

But we didn't have to wait long. Angel spoke up, "I don't think we should have borders either, that's just wrong. People should be able to do what they want."

"So what you are saying," I asked, "Is that you don't mind if strangers come into your house and eat your food, hangout in your living room. Sleep in your room. Is that right?"

Of course he didn't think and reacted right away, "That's not what I mean, people should have a right..."

"What?" Now an older man, John Wood was twisting in his chair. "You don't have a right for shit. You don't even belong in this country. Did you fire a weapon anywhere for the United States?"

Angel shrunk, so I helped him, "Angel, if you don't have walls for your house, do you have a house?"

"No. Not really."

"If you don't have borders for a country, do you have a country?"

He thought for a moment "No, but Trump's a racist."

That's all Angel had. Spoon-fed. So I asked, "Where did you hear that?"

"On TV. On the news."

"And you believe it? Have you met Trump? How do you know?"

"I guess, I guess I don't know."

There's NO QUESTION that Donald Trump is responsible for raising the problems of illegal immigration to the national stage. If it weren't for Trump, we wouldn't be talking about illegal immigration in a meaningful way, because few politicians have been brave enough to talk about it in depth, just an obligatory mention. With Trump, it has been an explosion into the topic, into the minds of all Americans, love him or hate him.

This is the quote about illegal immigration and that made worldwide headlines: "They're sending people that have lots of problems, and they're bringing those problems [to] us. They're bringing drugs. They're bringing crime. They're rapists. And some, I assume, are good people."

Reader, I want you to look closely at the above *edited* quote. It's a common feature in journalism to change a word to more accurately represent what the speaker meant by putting it in brackets. In this case it's [to], where Trump actually said "with." This edited version appears in many publications such as The Guardian, Business Insider, American Free Press, The Hill, and Chicago Sun-Times.

Trump received no such treatment on "They're rapists," or many other Trump quotes. So-called "journalists" instead had a field day, a field *year* actually. They used the out of context "They're rapists" to lambaste Trump with all sorts of hateful accusations against peoples and races.

If Trump had said the word "some" to begin, i.e. "Some of them are rapists," the firestorm about how Trump hates Mexicans (which he doesn't) would never have ensued from the media campaign arm which is CNN, and from the Hillary campaign itself.

Democrats and their celebrity supporters used "They're racists" selfishly to elevate their own stock. Actress America Ferrera wrote an open letter to Donald Trump, published on Huffington Post, thanking him for his "hateful rhetoric" about Mexican immigrants because it will energize Latino voters to vote for other candidates. (Which it largely didn't.)

"Remarks like yours will serve brilliantly to energize Latino voters and increase turnout on election day against you and any other candidate who runs on a platform of hateful rhetoric," Ferrera wrote.

During her DNC appearance on July 26, 2016, she said, "Donald's not making America great again, he's making America hate again. The vast majority of us cannot afford to see his vision of America come to be."

You see how unethical and anti-progress this is? TAKING ADVANTAGE and FULLY LICENTIOUS of word twisting and the emotions of the uninformed?

Of course, no sane person believes that all Mexicans who cross an American border are rapists. This defies logic. But did the media react responsibly? No. And because of the frequent dishonesty by the press, voters gradually ignored the one-line zingers presented on TV and began going online to watch Trump's entire speeches and responses. Sensible people began to see full well what Donald meant, and they shared it with their friends.

Today's media is like a hawk waiting for something in the brush to make a mistake. For a human being, this is cowardly and dishonest. I am personally ashamed of many biased journalists who massage information and bank that you won't question further. Trump's calling out of these improprieties gained traction into Election Day as a growing number of Americans distrusted their own people countrymen that worked in the media.

The battle between what was truthfully expressed and what the media wants you to believe has drained America's patience with the "news." For some it's a total hatred. Many people have sworn off CNN like a disease, as well as other news organizations that proved their equity bias for Hillary Clinton.

The media's effort to fluff away Trump by accusing him of hating Mexicans and subsequently charging him as an all-out racist, was a pivotal and tragic moment in American history. Journalism died. People began to wise up and search for the truth of the matter.

Maybe some good will come of it, perhaps an enlightenment of ethical standards. Will journalism professors offer their students something new? So that reporters won't violate the much stomped on Journalist's Creed? How will we deal with new participants in media: Twitter, Facebook, bloggers, and fake news sites? Will vice win? Money! Greed! Exposure! Fame! The wolves in the "real world" are always lying in wait to test the graduates.

The concern for The Trump House here is two-fold. One is the fact that Donald is passionate about securing our nation's border, and second, that after countless "wash and spin" attempts at twisting Trump's words to paint him as an anti-Person, people are weary of the media's manipulation of public figures.

Mitt Romney received the "racist treatment" when the democrats saw that he was progressing. A long line of republican opponents have been accused of either being a racist, a Nazi, or a misogynist by the Democratic Party, when in fact, according to Roger L. Simon, 90% of the racism in America comes from the Democratic Party and the Left.

Why does racism prevail politically? Why does it really exist? Two camps, fear, and business.

The phony narrative of racism dominates our media landscape. Everyone knows that there's unfairness in all aspects of humanity, but also that racism has *become a business!* If you don't believe this, ask yourself why CNN perpetuates the same racist accusations and conversations over and over again. Why? Because sensationalism sells advertising slots on television.

It's a business. Why don't you ask Robert L. Johnson, who founded BET (Black Entertainment Television). He believed in racism so much that he made a killing from it, $3 billion to be exact. This is what Viacom paid him for ownership of BET, because they too thought racism was a good revenue stream. Check FUBU. Movies, sneakers, books, hoodies, car wheels, food, and talk show hosts who make a killing pitting one race against the other. Just about every rich rapper out there has racism to thank. And how many more books and movies and songs do we need about racism? As if we don't have enough recorded history of racism to remind us.

Angel and I had a short talk later that day. I reminded him that many people come into the U.S. who aren't wanted in their own country, because they are criminals, and that their country doesn't want their crimes or to pay the cost of supporting the convict in prison.

"Uh-huh. I don't believe that."

I told him about the 64-year-old California woman who was brutally raped by an illegal alien from Mexico. Victor Ramirez was arrested four times in two years, deported five times. I told Angel the woman died eight days later.

"Yeah?"

Then I told him about Kate Steinle, also in California, who was killed by a homeless illegal alien, Juan Lopez-Sanchez, also deported five times, who fired a stolen gun that caught Kate, an innocent 32-year-old beautiful woman, in the back. She died two hours later.

"I didn't never hear about these women, these cases."

"You play too much poker. Every time I come here, you're here."

"Nah, I just like it, that's all," he laughed.

"You should like getting informed. Read something once in a while."

"I'll try to read up on it. I won't accuse anything without the facts, or before thinking about it. I like that you talk to me."

"That's good." I said. "You're too young to begin wrong, to let people on TV make up your mind for you."

"As long as they don't send me back."

"Have you committed any crimes?"

"No."

"Don't worry, you won't be among the first to go."

He laughed, but then his face grew serious just before he went through the door, still looking at me.

Illegal immigration was brought to the top of the American Conversation by Donald Trump. The proposal that it has no place in American society is a huge brick in The Trump House.

DEATH TO AMERICA

It might as well be death to the entire planet if ISIS gets their way.

Like my father said, a day after September 11, 2001 when the Twin Towers were destroyed and 3000 Americans with them, "These half-wits want to send us back to the 6th century." It's true.

With the exception of my father weighing in so accurately, I don't feel comfortable treating this part of the story with anecdotes or a personal experience, so we will get right to the heart of the matter.

Other than nuclear, ISIS is the single most dangerous threat to the American way of life, the European way of life, the Asian way of life, to every innocent country and their people, and the progress of mankind as a whole.

To be clear, the members of ISIS believe in their death cult. There are probably a few leaders at the top of ISIS calling the shots who live a life of luxury, who are laughing at the very soldiers that do their bidding. It keeps them in power, and they aren't moral as we know it. But perhaps these select leaders don't live in a brainwash like the minions of ISIS do. They just dole it out.

I'm not an ISIS member, so it is very difficult to place my mind there. I believe people across America have tried, on some level, to understand what possesses people to commit atrocities against their own people and against us, half a world away.

ISIS commits crimes against the planet. I am a nationalist, and it pains me to see cultured European countries suffering terrorist attacks as much as it does in our own country. I have enjoyed many cultures, it makes our population rich, with quality and interest. History. Learning.

But now the times are here where a dangerous ISIS ideology has taken hold, once again, just like the Nazi Party in Germany 1933-45, where the people that believe in it are trying to force it upon all people.

If you personally believe that America would be the stopping point for this cancer, by happenstance or luck, think again. ISIS will not be satisfied until it has conquered all peoples and nations, and still it won't be satisfied until it then turns on itself and kills itself. (Germany would have certainly turned on Japan if their partnership had been successful, and then toward its own people.) This is how insane the doctrine is, it doesn't really know where it's going. ISIS members are blind to "causes," although they believe in them til death. For death.

Once those causes are burned up, new dunderheads would move in, change the theme around, probably use a similar age-old text that is disprovable, paint up an icon to worship, and the cycle would carry on. I believe that ISIS isn't even aware of what it is doing. This is a provocative statement - stay with me.

The ISIS leaders, you can't know their minds, so this is part speculation. I say that no one group of a vast number is so roundly agreed in their motive. As a comparison, hardly ANY of the generals in the Nazi party truly believed in Hitler and his quest for world domination. In fact, Hitler had an affection for the British people and, in an amazing duality, he fired rockets into Britain and killed more civilians than British soldiers during some months of the war.

The youth of Germany, some were forced, but many were taken in by the promise of glory and strength, via propaganda. That is the key. Get them while they are young. This is what ISIS is doing now. Much like members of the Hitler Youth, many children in the Middle East madrassas learn a loathing for America that is wholly fabricated and implanted in their minds.

Yet the question remains. Why?

A young American today might reply, "Hitler was sick. He was insane. ISIS is sick. They don't believe in anything. They twist religion for their own cause."

Has ISIS hijacked a religion? Are they sick? Are the motives just a side-effect of a more out of control system, mindless cause and effect, handed down for centuries? For goodness' sake, what if Muhammad had never appeared in a biblical text? Or was named "T-bill." What other figurehead would ISIS use? What if Hitler's given last name of Schickelgruber was used and we got, "Heil Schickelgruber!" That wouldn't work. Firstly, the powerful alliteration is gone, and even Germans though it was a laughable name.

Adolf Schickelgruber changed his name to his father's name of Hitler after seeing what was in store for him with a name like that. Schickelgruber was Adolf's grandmother's surname, which was given to Adolf since his father was born out of wedlock, a deep taboo regarding honor in the German family. And... Hitler wasn't even German, but Austrian. Hitler had been a painter on the streets of Vienna who became... one of the worlds most notorious murderers. That makes sense, right? ISIS exclaims a love for God. That also makes sense, since they want to kill anyone who thinks differently than they do. Right?

I assert that they don't think rationally at all, not like we do. An ideological madness is out of control, or on autopilot. You can't know with certainty why terrorists act, what the motives are in the chain of command. But you can see things add up in a chain of events. That happens daily. And the media loves to put it together for you on television so that you come back the next day and watch some more commercials and buy a lot of prescription medication that you don't need.

I submit, even with the available history of ISIS, al-Qaeda, Boko Haram, and all terrorists, given everything that the experts have offered up, and the testaments left behind by self-exploded terrorists, ISIS is a movement that knows what it is doing only insomuch as it rides on the material its leaders feed to those who are willing, or forced, to follow.

Was Bin Laden a true believer in jihad? Probably. But how can you know? Maybe he was apathetic about life and saw no path to feeling good, and so, in a sickness, Bin Laden exorcised his griefs on a target that would allow him to keep doing that just that, supported by the people he so easily manipulated. WE CAN'T KNOW. And I say, IT DOESN'T MATTER.

What matters is that we kill them. Then we eradicate the cancer off the planet through education. Trying to understand motive and being politically correct while airplanes are crashing into our buildings and guns are firing off in clubs and bombs exploding at marathon races and knives are stabbing at our students on U.S. college campuses will only get us more of the same. Perhaps parts of the planet's population has not caught up with the civilized world, not entirely because of economic regress, but because mankind hasn't been on the planet long enough to know how to handle itself, given the swift rise of technology, wholly unbalanced by the inability for many people to control their emotions.

Now is the time for action. Donald Trump knows this. He asserted straightaway in his first campaign speech, "Nobody will be tougher on ISIS than Donald Trump. Nobody. I will find within our military, I will find the General Patton, or I will find General MacArthur, I will find the right guy to take that military and make it really work. Nobody will be pushing us around."

ISIS depends largely on Iran's assistance. In 2012, our Treasury Department uncovered financial ties between Iran and al-Qaeda in Iraq (AQI). This is the terrorist group that evolved into ISIS. This we *know*. It is likely that broad financial ties have existed between them for years. Does this information help us understand? Given the state of the world coming now at a fast pitch, it only matters what they are *doing*.

Iran has cleverly taken advantage of the weak Obama Administration and is now on the path to nuclear armament. Some of our top generals agree, despite assurances of containment from the Obama Administration. Retired U.S. Army Maj. Gen. Paul Vallely believes Iran *already has* nuclear weapons and that the U.S. government knows about it.

In an August, 2015 interview with wnd.com, Vallely said that President Obama, Secretary of State John Kerry, and Senior Adviser Valerie Jarret, "Are treading on treason under the U.S. Constitution for aiding and abetting Iran, a known enemy of the U.S., while throwing Israel, a longtime U.S. ally, to the wolves."

Iran and Palestine have openly stated that, "Israel doesn't have a right to exist." How will this be reconciled? Would Iran stop with Israel or send some missiles to the U.S. too? I think you know the answer.

How do you feel about Obama giving to the enemy, Iran, who chants "Death To America" at Friday prayers, $33B in cash and gold? How do you feel about this? Since cash is the currency of terrorism.

Donald Trump is ready. Ready to further develop and enact his national security plan. And while details change and circumstances fluctuate, the following is true: Children can be manipulated easily. Part of the world is out of control. Particular regimes are taking advantage of their young. The motives matter only if they help us defeat all terrorists - not to *understand* and give them a hug. Wake up. They want to kill us.

We can't have "Death to America" on this planet in light of our Founding Fathers who were so brilliant as to set up and enact a government for the benefit of all people, when mindless terrorists want to hurdle us back to the 6th century.

Donald Trump wants to crush ISIS. People believe him. I believe him. The confidence that the

American people have in President-Elect Trump and in the American Military to successfully rid the world of this cancer is another major brick in The Trump House. God Bless America.

R-R-R-RAW POWER

Julian Assange, the founder of Wikileaks and a dealer of information that he believes populations need to know about their governments, remarked in an interview about his own life, "I don't go out. I am losing sense of time, and feeling very much detached from the world."

Isn't it ironic that one of the most powerful pieces in the chess game that was the 2016 Presidential Campaign couldn't move more than 50 yards from his residence at any time, for fear of certain arrest?

The irony highlights the presidential contest: the unconventional versus the all-powerful Democratic Machine. A David and Goliath story, or rather, two Davids and one Goliath. Julian Assange and Donald Trump versus Hillary Clinton.

Nobody saw this match up coming. There was a clue when Trump set a record and won every county in Pennsylvania in the Republican Primary, earning 89 of the 93 delegates. This was a leading indicator, and when I personally took strict notice. "If he can do all that," I thought, "if that many people are responding to Trump's calling our leaders incompetent and stupid, the whole country could come along."

I remember vividly, as most people do when there's a significant world event, I was walking across a casino floor, in Pennsylvania, and there were 20 televisions on the walls with Trump's big confident face and a banner, "Trump usurps Ted Cruz and John Kasich in Tuesday's crucial Pennsylvania primary."

I watched the entire piece. The reporter closed it with Trump remarking, "It's crazy what's going on, if I win, I still might not get the ballot. We have to give it back to the voters. But I think we are going to do well, look at the crowds."

When the primary win was reported on April 26, 2015 you could feel the change where people gathered. At work, at the casino, on social media. Groups formed in support of Trump. People came together and new friendships formed. Families also began to argue. Couples that I knew broke up. There was something new in the air. Trump. Trump. Trump. Everyone was talking Trump, love him or hate him, and this is when I began to hear on certain AM Radio programs Donald referred to as "The Trumpster."

The Trump campaign took on a new personality, different than the fun and glory gained by pigeoning his competitors with catchy names such as "Lyin' Ted" and "Low Energy Jeb." Up to the primary it had been a stage game of defining an opponent. But with the win tucked under his belt, Trump had a seemingly endless level of energy for rallies, internet participation, and a loyal staff that was very resourceful. All of which the DNC tried to convince you otherwise. In fact, as a whole, the Hillary campaign pandered to the uninformed, hoping voters would lead with their hearts on their sleeves and trust snippets of stories taken out of context, instead of doing their own research. As the days flipped by and Wikileaks produced, the American people began to distrust CNN, ABC and Hillary's speeches and debates. Gradually, people became thirsty for entire stories, the facts. The uninformed became the informed. Wikileaks hasn't published an inaccurate piece in 10 years.

The DNC also erroneously focused a negative campaign on Trump's tweets, which brought more attention to his pathway of talking to the American voters. Followers of Trump grew daily by the thousands. With Twitter, any news that Trump wanted to share couldn't be watered down or reinterpreted. Trump realized the value in direct communication very early in the game.

Trump was fast becoming a leader of the American people. He won TN, VT, FL GA, VA, etc., but winning every county in PA and setting a voter record there was an important brick in The Trump House. This is when people began to believe he could win the Presidency. Hopeful supporters got a huge upgrade and hard core supporters became more entrenched, and the presidency became tangible.

After the conclusion of Democratic Primary, Julian Assange published a collection of Democratic National Committee emails on July 22, 2016. If you ever, as a kid, tossed mud globs at a bee's nest under the eaves of an apartment building, you would know what it's like to be a member of the DNC on that day.

The email content ranged from disenfranchising Bernie Sanders from his proper treatment in the DNC, lack of confidence in Hillary Clinton, what news organizations to build relationships with, who hated who, and some emails even questioned Hillary's sanity. And so began the long days of Wikileak suffering at the

Hillary campaign, the beginning of "Death By A Thousand Cuts."

The DNC was hoping against hope, and kept their candidate alive. Have you seen the Steve McQueen movie, "The Sand Pebbles." There's a scene where the locals have captured a perceived traitor and from the shoreline they have him tied up in a noose-like fashion. He's alive, but one-by-one citizens come forward with a blade and give him a cut. Steve McQueen's character looks on helpless, but quickly he snatches a rifle and mercifully shoots his captured and tortured friend to spare him the "Death By A Thousand Cuts."

They didn't do anything like that over at the DNC. Hillary remained on life support. They didn't give Bernie Sanders any satisfaction as far as delegates either. You can't go back in time, so what could you do? This was the big trick played by the DNC on their constituents and the America people, defrauding Bernie and clinging to Hillary.

Although the DNC Chair, Debbie Wasserman, was forced to resign, revealed by Wikileaks that she had been tipping the race toward Hillary Clinton, it was a token gesture. Wasserman received another job from Hillary speedy quick, as honorary chair of her 50-state program.

Still, the bee-stung and lacerated Hillary Camp didn't act wisely on new information. It was like putting band aids on wounds made by a machine gun. The DNC didn't exercise what would have been a prudent move, to induct a full-stop and nominate a new candidate such as Senator Sanders or Vice President Joe Biden. Many top level democrats wanted to do this but Hillary wouldn't let go. Too many of her faithfuls believed, in a brainwash perhaps, that she simply *deserved* the presidency, just for repeatedly showing up. Hubster Bill Clinton thought so too. He said so at a private fundraiser in October 2015 in Chesapeake, MD. Another fact, compliments of Wikileaks.

What did the unearthing of these facts mean? Aside of moneymaking political gossip? What about these juicy details, bandied about by everyone from bellhop to bank executive? Does it sounds like a market top? The top for Hillary?

This is what it meant:

Do you remember R-R-R-RAW POWER? Circa 1975. This was a bicycle handlebar attachment that simulated the sound of a motorcycle. It was fun and actually sounded cool. It didn't do anything for your bike's performance, but Ideal sold a lot of them. The key thing was that kids in the neighborhood could hear you coming. It wasn't as envious as having a new 10-speed that older kids had, or a big Green Machine for the spoiled brat at the end of the street. It was a signature that you were a little bit cool, that your bicycle chain didn't always fall off, or you weren't poor. Whatever. The point here is that I was struck, waking up one morning in the midst of writing this book, and there it was - a signal.

Wikileaks is R-R-R-RAW POWER, leading the charge, Trump was coming up the block to kick some ass. The secluded Assange and the ubiquitous Trump revealed unprecedented corruption in American politics, and it tore into the Hillary campaign such that they couldn't recover.

Trump and Wikileaks became an unstoppable force. But is this right? Perhaps the mystery revealed is the inverse, that the carry through of the Wikileaks and Trump message are bona fide facts, but only that. Perhaps they served as a vehicle for the underlying truth, which is that the American people reached out, having now the accurate information they deserved all along. Today's environment for public treatment is not like it was in the early 1970s when the Tricky Dick Squad or other deceptive groups could bury information in a media without an internet.

Wikileaks was just beginning for Hillary, and really, so was Donald Trump. Trump became Trump after winning the primary, much like Rush, the rock band, didn't become Rush with the first album but with *Moving Pictures*. Great wine takes time. Trump was learning, and learning fast. At this point, a very solid Wiki/Trump cornerstone was set in The Trump House.

Don't forget the R-R-R-RAW POWER.

LOCK BEANPOLE HILLARY UP!

YOU are irredeemable. At least 25% of you, did you know that? If you blob all the American people into one, your leg, arm, and another portion of your body is BEYOND HOPE! BEYOND HELP! You can't learn. You are so bad, we dismiss you.

Here's Hillary, September 9, 2016, two months before election day, sticking her neck into the guillotine, although she thought she was being cute and getting votes while sucking up to a small group of donors who paid an estimated $25,000 to hear her talk.

"You could put half of Trump's supporters into what I call, The Basket of Deplorables." (Laughter) "Right? They're racist, sexist, homophobic, xenophobic, islamophobic, you name it."

Meanwhile, *STRONGER TOGETHER* hovers just in front of her.

Hillary continued, "Now some of those folks, they are irredeemable, but thankfully, they are not America."

Um, if you were a Hillary supporter and you are reading this, understand with this moment, Hillary lost a significant number of votes.

When Americans heard this, a sinker fell in their stomachs. Enough of this woman. Her condemnation of people alone was enough to turn away any voter, but Hillary felt the need to qualify the next day. She tweeted, "I regret saying "half." This turned off people even more! When I read her tweet I couldn't help but laugh. Some apology.

Hillary's Deplorable Moment was... very strange. I thought that maybe Hillary was subconsciously trying to sabotage her own campaign. Maybe she didn't want to be president. She wants the title, but not the work. That much I believe is true.

The event was strange in that it provided for real parsing of Hillary's failures over many years. How do I say this... of course many people for different reasons have been dissatisfied with Hillary for a long time, but now EVERYONE was paying attention, because of the Deplorable Accusation. This led to relentless exposition of her greatest sins, lies, and failures.

They are:

Hillary has taken money from countries that throw gays off buildings.

Hillary lied about a terrorist attack that killed four Americans in Benghazi, claiming a YouTube video incited the violence. Her motive was to prevent a known terrorist attack on the anniversary of 9/11 hurt the re-election of Obama.

The Clinton Foundation "charity" takes money countries that don't allow women to drive. Every part of their body must be covered but their eyes. Marital rape is legal. Hillary claims she is a feminist.

Hillary destroyed laptops, cellphones, federal documents, and deleted emails after a Congressional Subpoena instructed her to cease and desist.

Hillary promised to keep Attorney General Loretta Lynch if she is elected president only days after Bill Clinton and Loretta met in the back The Lynch Plane.

Hillary lied to the FBI saying she never received or sent any classified material on her private server.

Hillary has stated, "It was allowed," about her email practices.

Hillary lied and stated that all her grandparents immigrated to America. Only one did.

Hillary claimed in an interview, "We came out of the White House not only dead broke, but in debt. We struggled to piece together the resources for mortgages for houses, for Chelsea's education. It wasn't easy..."

The Clinton's captured $153M without providing a service or a product, from 2001 until May 2016. These monies were paid by Goldman Sachs, CitiGroup, Morgan Stanley, Bank of America, and UBS. Other speech fees were "trimmed" from foreign lobbyists who sought a meeting with Secretary of State Hillary Clinton, disguised as speaking fees paid to Bill, who brought in the lion's share at $132M - a perfect fence for brokering State Department favors and Wall Street pals. Toss in the $200,000/year president's salary.

Yes, it has worried many Americans that the Clinton's might not be able to scrape up enough money to purchase a "lil' Clinton shack of their own" down by the river, after years of excellent service to the country. Thank God they saved their pennies and were able to pay the $1.7M price for their new property in Chappaqua, NY.

Hillary appears to be a liar in a class of her own. Have we ever had a politician get away with so much crime and insult to the American people?

Judge Jeanine Pirro of Fox News put it this way, "Hillary you are a liar! And a pathological one at that. You are a cheat, dishonest, condescending, you are arrogant, contemptuous, and if you think that your half-assed apology will wipe the slate clean, you are wrong... I can't trust a president who doesn't think that I'm not worthy of being an American." (Fox News averages 2.2M viewers a night in prime time.)

Trump's running mate Governor Mike Pence responded, "She referred to those people as 'irredeemable,'" he said, at the Values Voter Summit in Washington, D.C. "Well I will tell you right now, I campaign on a regular basis with Donald Trump. I campaign all across this country for Donald Trump. Hillary Clinton's low opinion of the people who support this campaign should be denounced in the strongest possible terms.

"The people who support Donald Trump's campaign are hard-working Americans," Pence added. "Let me just say from the bottom of my heart: Hillary, they are not a basket of anything, they are Americans and they deserve your respect.

"No one with a record of failure at home and abroad, no one with her avalanche of dishonesty and corruption, and no one with that low opinion of the American people should ever be elected president of the United States of America," he said.

Despite this heat, Hillary's Deplorable Moment was soon eclipsed by another voter-losing moment only two days later. It was the "I've fallen down and I can't get up without the help of my secret service" moment.

After leaving a 9/11 ceremony early, claiming to be light headed from heat exposure, while the temperature was 79 degrees and 54 percent humidity, the whole world watched as Hillary waited unbalanced for her van to arrive. She stepped forward, loses a shoe, and while bent at the knees was caught as she fell forward and assisted into the van.

Later that afternoon came an announcement that she was diagnosed with pneumonia. Soon after, she was let out for everyone to see, walking on the sidewalk, talking and taking pictures with a young girl.

The campaign knew that Hillary had pneumonia, and possibly another medical condition related to seizures. Indeed, Wikileaks revealed that Hillary's assistants searched the internet for "seizure medication," Provigil in particular.

The enormous failing in responsibility to disclose this to the American voter is another fantastic lie, in a box, in another box of lies. From one box to the other, it was becoming apparent that the level of distrust for Hillary Clinton was reaching a new high. American's thirst for rule of law and moral imperatives returning to Washington D.C. via Trump was now a significant part of the national conversation.

Hillary was becoming her own albatross. You could feel it. People across America were starting to realize that she might not even be physically capable of doing the job of president. And so it went, Donald on the other side of the track, gaining votes, talking directly to the American people, while Hillary's lies and failures were adding up to voters going somewhere else. The truth about votes in this election is not so much that Trump won, but that *Hillary lost*. Hillary helped Hillary lose the election.

No magic beans, such as: calling Americans deplorable, hauling out 12 phony accounts of sexual assault against Trump, ginning up to the biggest banks in America, "pressing against" AG Loretta Lynch, or even paying Bob Creamer to sabotage Trump rallies, would work.

Hillary Clinton was out of beanstalk to climb. She never got past 50% of the country's support, although she was expected to win by a landslide, according to all the phony and paid "pollsters." All the lies and crimes, a side of the game that knows no genuine forgiveness, was pointing back to Hillary alone, and the American people didn't like what they saw. Fifty-one percent of Trump voters maintained that part of their reason in choosing Trump was because they didn't trust Hillary.

Hillary's self-destruction and distaste for her by the American voter, are important bricks in The Trump House.

LAUGHING LORETTA LYNCH
AND LOVERBOY BILL CLINTON

De' plane Boss! It's de' plane! No, this isn't Tattoo from Fantasy Island, it's Bill Clinton having a Romp Fest in the back of Loretta Lynch's airplane at Sky Harbor Airport on June 29, 2016.

Bill and Loretta were kickin' it with "Pomp and Circumstance" playing in the background, but "Caught Me Riding Dirty" was soon playing in the minds of the American voter.

Loretta Lynch is Attorney General for the USA appointed by President Obama, and formerly appointed by Bill Clinton in 1999 as lead U. S. Attorney until 2001. Bosom Buddies? Not the Tom Hanks version, but the Capone kind.

What was said on the Lynch plane? Does it matter, the exact words? Common sense tells us what happened. This was the beginning of the Skate For Free party over in the Hillary camp, and the democrats believed that Bill's success on the plane was a hard thrust forward of the line of scrimmage. But the American people didn't appreciate the secret meeting. Ethical people don't like it when world leaders behave deceptively. Farmers don't like it. Factory workers don't like it.

Managers of banks don't like it. The girl behind the counter at WaWa didn't like it when I asked her. "She punched the cash register and said, "I hate her!"

Perhaps the only hard thrust forward was Bill giving it to Loretta Lynch. In the back of the plane! How sweet! I mean, that's possible. Right? Given Bill Clinton's track record of infidelity. Can you hear it now, with his trousers down, "You, will, not, prosecute, my wife," while Loretta loves it, or hates it. Who knows. If only we had a Loretta Lynch dress like the Lewinsky dress. DNA and all.

But it wasn't DNA on Bill's mind that day on the tarmac, it was the DNC. But the DNC didn't see in their arrogance a conviction taking hold in the voters' minds that Hillary was not to be trusted. Despite Bill and Loretta's magical love fest, by all appearances, Hillary was a star and would *remain one*. That was the perception they wanted to project - Hillary was more of a star, now that honey Bill played an ace and cashed in a debt owed by Loretta Lynch. And the po-li-ti-kay surrounding the democrats were in a state of glee, because they believed they would get away with it. And they did, at least in the legal world. Now perceived by most Americans as - the illegal world.

Let's talk plainly. Days after "Lovin' Loretta and Bangin' Bill," FBI Director James Comey announced on June 6 that while Hillary was guilty of gross negligence and "extremely careless in their handling of very sensitive, highly classified information... no reasonable prosecutor would bring such a case."

Everyone I know, was floored. All the legal experts (except pro-Hillary) on TV, were aghast. The hundreds of investigators over at the FBI were beside themselves, embarrassed. Soon we would find out to what degree by the high number of resignations threatened and laid on James Comey's desk.

Hillary Clinton owned and operated a private server at her personal residence in Chappaqua, NY, deliberately circumventing departmental infrastructure and policy, whereupon classified information was sent and received from it. It put U.S. national security at risk beyond measure. She destroyed evidence under subpoena. She lied to the FBI. All these actions are federal high crimes.

For all these crimes she was given a pass, and apart from most die hard Hillary supporters, the American people were furious. Trump supporters were red hot, ready to take up arms, literally and with the vote. Trump rallies were getting bigger and the law was getting weaker. A powerful combination.

Anger was swelling in the hearts of American's for the double standard treatment that Hillary received. "Lock her up!" was becoming a national slogan.

There's a visceral reaction across all fellow countrymen who feel betrayed. Abandoned. Told law is only for common folk. Told that their vote is insignificant if not cast for Hillary. A true hatred was growing for Hillary and her people.

On a broad scale, populations will suffer large drags on it's resources, on its integrity, on its neediness or even stealth by governments, as long as people can function and take care of their families, or at least have a path of hope toward that. As long as there is a ballot of fairness or maybe pieces of any of these that add up to a livable life - people accept it.

But there's a limit. It's like when a 5 year-old doesn't want to eat liver, and there's nothing you can do about it. Even onions and ketchup won't help. No, it's more like when a murderer is let out of jail after serving four years and kills again. Like the Clinton's 30-year crime spree! When a GROSS

INJUSTICE is placed on the American people and they revolt inside, feeling genuinely hurt, you get that revolution. Here is a TV word I have tried to avoid, but it's correct - repudiation. A full table flip.

The Frankenstein that had become the Clintons would no longer be tolerated. Republican registration and absentee ballots soared across the country, most notably in Florida, North Carolina, Iowa, and Nevada, and broke many records. Twitter users were flocking to Trump's twitter account by the millions. Trump had 15.8M followers on election night. He has 1.1M more today, and growing.

Laughing Loretta and Bang Boy Bill might have thought that they were doing Hillary and the democrats a great service, but it backfired, despite that THE LAW was not the law.

The law did not serve the people. But the people served themselves by voting away from corruption, and toward the promise of justice and America values. The rejection of Loretta Lynch's failure to act in the best interest of the United States was a key brick put in place by the American people, in The Trump House.

KELLYANNE CONWAY

Is Kellyanne Conway the coolest cucumber under fire? Isn't it fun just to say her name! Many of the pundits and TV hosts didn't think so after their repeated attempts failed to unnerve her and have her spout off about Trump in some unexpected manner.

In just about every interview after August 17, 2016, the day Trump hired Kellyanne as his Campaign Manager, the tone and aggression toward Kellyanne was noticeably ratcheted up and, to be blunt, unfriendly. Before this day, CNN panelists and hosts had been operating on a debatable equality. TV hosts included her as a peer, not a target. Don't be fooled by the intermittent casual tone of any of these hosts, it's like a radar behind the curtain, waiting for some slip in words or a weakness in demeanor to pounce on Kellyanne, and then to denigrate Trump.

A super-rich example of a CNN hatchet job foiled by Kellyanne occurred just after the November 5, 2016 "ruckus," for lack of a better word, in Reno, NV. A Hillary supporter, Austin Crites, went into the crowd and either he or people near him shouted "Gun! Gun!" Trump was rushed off stage and Crites escorted away. Trump returned moments later, in Trump-like fashion.

(Side note: The only reason Trump bailed out of a Chicago rally on May 6, 2015 was because "protesters" paid by the Hillary campaign were in full form and inciting violence. People could have died, and there was no admonishment by the press or investigation by the FBI.)

So Jake Tapper at CNN gives treatment to the possible assassination attempt on Trump by running this headline, "Trump campaign tweeting misinformation about Nevada incident." Let's pause here. Really? What about the guy with the alleged gun? THE HILLARY SUPPORTER WHO WHEN INTO A TRUMP CROWD AND CAUSED TROUBLE!

Jake asks, "So first of all, we're glad everyone is okay." Then without pausing for breath, "I have to ask, your social media director... Should they be spreading this misinformation?"

Kellyanne doesn't hesitate, "I'm glad you're happy that everyone is okay. That's the main focus here. All the coverage is usually about our protesters wreaking havoc and making people feel afraid, and this certainly goes both ways." And later in the same response, "I also want to point out that... [Crites] had canvassed for Hillary Clinton and he had donated to her campaign. So this is a Democratic plant or operative trying to disrupt our rally. People saw a nimble and resilient Donald Trump who would be nimble and resilient as president, take back to the stage..."

Then Jake hits her again, "Why is your campaign spreading that it was [an assassination attempt]?"

"First of all," replies Kellyanne, "that's really remarkable... that this is the story line here." *That this is the story line.*

What is also remarkable is that Kellyanne always remains on top of the relevancy of an issue, all the while unflappable.

CNN gets high marks for fabrication and spin. Statistically. If you plotted their irresponsible moments on a bar graph, theirs would be a line shooting off the chart. The media bias for Hillary Clinton was so pervasive that even the respected, last stop of good journalism, the BBC, got infected. The BBC interviewed only Hillary supporters in many instances and poked fun at Trump with words like "antics" and "pantomime" as a brush off, just before broadcasting a positive piece on Hillary.

Throughout Kellyanne's role as Campaign Manager for Trump, she remained consistent and positive for all people, championing that "the voters will speak." Never throwing a barb unless to respond, a jab by Kellyanne was still rare. This is the tactical gem, to have an advocate so visible and grounded. A professional.

She also carries a gem of humanity in her work. On the day Trump hired her, she was interviewed by The Washington Post and had this for listeners, "For what purpose?"

Here's her full reply to the Washington Post, "Part of why [Trump] ended up running this time as opposed to all the times he flirted with it and did not, is because people called him a circus act, a clown, a joke. For what purpose? First of all, it's not that nice. Secondly, who are some of these 22-year-old bloggers that work for unprofitable outlets insulting a guy who employs 22,000 people and has made something of his life? So if you want to treat someone a certain way, maybe you better ignore them next time, because, as my grandmother used to say, be careful what you wish for."

Kellyanne has a natural talent to distill to the usefulness, or uselessness, of a motive. I've watched hundreds of Kellyanne videos and followed her throughout the campaign. She get's to the heart of the matter quickly.

Kellyanne is a "philosophers and friends first" kind of gal. But make no mistake, she carries a big hammer, armed with the facts, statistics, and a sharp intuition. She is always prepared, always decent and friendly. Even when conversations become arguments, she's like a light bulb that never flickers. It's enjoyable to watch, not solely because she wins, but mostly because she maintains her integrity and sense of fairness. She's a good human being.

This has been the media side of Kellyanne's job. Kellyanne Conway is a also a professional pollster. She is the CEO of The Polling Company Inc./Woman Trend, and advised Trump years before on whether or not he would be competitive in a presidential election. Fast forward to 2015 and Kellyanne is working for a Ted Cruz super PAC, Keep the Promise 1, before being hired by Trump. Now she is the first woman to have run a Republican presidential campaign.

Polling data in Bucks and Montgomery counties in Pennsylvania, last minute polls in Michigan and key counties in Florida translated by

Conway helped Trump get where he needed to be. Her polls were major factors in earning votes and spreading the Trump message. It is difficult to go behind the scenes when you are not a pollster, but it's hours of data collection and synthesis to arrive at an actionable conclusion. It decides what part of your message appeals to that voter, and how relevant that area of the country is in relation to your opponent, who also wants those votes.

Elections are about winning, unfortunately there's a ruthless mathematical side to it. Appealing to a voter and sharing the message is paramount. With this unavoidably rigid approach you must instruct your nominee with cold facts, and likewise determine the weaknesses of your opponent.

Kellyanne rose to this challenge and brought a perspective which wasn't obvious to the world. She understood that the democrats were not prepared for the possibility of a Trump win, that they didn't have a grasp on the concerns of the American people. This was key. It won votes. It kept he campaign on the best course.

Kellyanne has come to be known as "The Trump Whisperer." She certainly has his ear and guided him to keep on message. She advised him how messy "unorthodox" expressions can become inside the media (unfairly), and employing the teleprompter to ensure that the Make America Great Again message was heard accurately.

If Trump had his way... maybe... Consider the facts that Trump has a nice family, he's a father, a grandfather, and, as much as the media wants to paint him as a tyrant, he isn't. He's just assertive. But for the art of illustration, let me put it this way: If Trump had his way, he would hit the audience over the head with an 8-inch thick bible, pay attention! This is what I mean! America is in trouble! And no available tool of expression would be off limits. People actually love Trump for shades of this.

With Kellyanne Conway as part of the Trump team, fending off the vultures in the media, providing accurate and meaningful polling information, and being an all-around bright light of guidance and friendship, Kellyanne is a major brick in building The Trump House.

SCAFFOLDING

It's hard to build a big house without scaffolding.

I put at the midpoint here the list of campaign promises Donald J. Trump made to the American people during his first campaign speech on June 16, 2015 as candidate for President of the United States.

Repeal and replace Obamacare

Build a wall on our southern border

Defeat ISIS

Stop Iran from getting nuclear weapons

Immediately terminate Obama's executive order on immigration

Fully support 2nd amendment

End Common Core

Rebuild America's infrastructure (under budget and on time)

Save Medicare, Medicaid, and Social Security (without cuts)

Renegotiate foreign trade deals

Reduce our $18T debt

Strengthen the United States Military

Take care of our veterans

After watching countless Donald Trump interviews and rallies (many at over capacity while supporters gathered in the parking lots) I didn't witness any vacancy in his personality that would translate to him not getting results. Trump has proven results in business. He comes across as a man who will get the job done. Let us help our president achieve his goals.

Trump: "We have all the cards. But we don't know how to use them. We don't even know that we have the cards. Because our leaders don't understand the game."

BLACK POWER

Black power. Yes. What is it? Like anything, it is defined by what it does. What did black power do in this election? Where did it come from exactly? Did it come from the Obamas? Did it come from Black Lives Matter? Did it come from black celebrities? Did it come from the black inner city voters? Black policemen? Black news anchors?

Asking these question assumes that black power influenced the 2016 election. Did it? The word "power" also assumes by lack of qualification that black power was strong. It's easy to equate the word "power" with "strong." What about the other possibility? What about black weakness? Or rather, decisiveness, the decision to "stay put," and let the chips fall where they may.

All these were factors. The black vote was scattered all over the place relative to history. The important take is that when we examine where blacks put their vote, it's a leading indicator for upcoming change in America, what it means to be those black *and* white voters who are conscious of duty and our fellow men, each deserving the same human and civil rights as everybody.

So let's see what happened with black power and Donald Trump. Let's see where it came from and where it landed.

True black power, as many anticipated, did NOT come from President Obama during his two presidencies. If it had, Hillary Clinton would have been President-Elect of the USA with 52% of the vote. Obama nearly begged for Hillary votes, going so far to telling his base that it would be, "A personal insult," if they didn't activate and get out and vote!

What kind of man does this, in these words? Who is this president who offends his citizens by trying to blackmail them into action? Oh, I guess it's a politician who will suffer any indignity to win and leave behind an agenda that he wants you to see. Ego, the wrong kind of ego. Obama pleaded for votes out of desperation. It's disappointing after eight years as president that he feels the need to do this.

Obama won 96% of the black vote in 2008. But what did he do with it? What a heaven sent opportunity for President Obama! 2008! You are President of the United States! And you are black! You are a black man in charge of the country! It couldn't be any better to bring black and whites together, to really show love for mankind, to lift black people in economic and social equality, where ever it may be lacking, to show the world what a black man can do where once he was enslaved! It can't get any better! Don't squander it!

What happened? It's eight years later now. Look around. On Obama's watch, the JV Team, coined by Obama, has committed murder inside our country. ISIS is now inside our borders. The FBI is investigating ISIS suspects in all 50 states.

Chicago, Obama's hometown where he was a community organizer, has suffered more than 700 homicides in 2016, a record. You can pop to a video, "Blacks In Chicago Say Obama Worst President Ever." Poverty has risen across the USA, black home ownership is down, food stamps are up. On Obama's watch, health care costs have risen steadily and in some states more than 100%. This is after an Obama Campaign Promise that health care costs would decline, and that you could also keep your doctor, which is also false.

The list of failings is long and grew steadily while Obama played 270 games of golf. That's about 140 days of time. Almost half a year of his time in office!

That's too much time wasted when your country needs you, when your black voters need you and are suffering. Time wasted! There's no time to waste. Is it reasonable to think that if you were a black man elected President of the USA, and that the whole world was watching to see what you would do for the long oppressed blacks across the land, that you would kick ass each and every minute in office!

Nope. Golf. Martha's Vineyard. Hamptons. Lavish dinners. Vacations and who knows what Obama has been doing? Spending our tax dollars on the secret service and jet fuel to get to these golf games and vacations (appx: $44M in taxpayer cash for travel). Eight years and little to show when the canvas and landscape was so ripe for success! What a colossal failure for the first black president. To be clear, I am white and I wanted Obama to succeed big time. It didn't happen.

To be fair, there were two successes while Obama was in office, Bin Laden was killed. This should have happened years before, and while it occurred on Obama's watch, it's not as if he had a strategic role. All he did was answer the generals, "If you think it's him, go ahead." The soldiers did the rest.

Unemployment declined in the USA under Obama. This is true, and false. Service jobs increased while manufacturing jobs declined. The heart of American jobs continued to leave our country while Obama failed to protect the American worker.

The list of Obama's failings is long, but what is important in the 2016 election is that the aware Obama voter now voted for Trump. Black and white. Specifically with the black vote, many stayed home, finding Obama's rants about Hillary to be unappealing. The more cognizant black voter knows that President Obama did nothing to help the black community.

Let's not forget the Obama Apology Tour when he went around the world to various countries apologizing for the "Sins Of America."

I guess Obama didn't read William Shirer's, "The Rise and Fall of the Third Reich" and learn that the United States saved Earth from worldwide oppression.

At a minimum of paying attention, I guess Obama didn't watch the movie, "Saving Private Ryan" either. The landing at Normandy on D-day, portrayed in the opening twenty minutes of the movie, is not to be touched. It is a moment in history that is deserving of honor and respect around the globe and throughout human time for the sacrifices young men and women made, and for it's importance in preserving mankind (like the importance of the Pelopennesian War). For America's success in WWII to be ponied and diminished by Obama is one of the most shameful acts by a sitting president.

Why is this relevant to Donald Trump winning, beyond the obvious want for a change of the guard? We have people like Sean Combs, also known as P. Diddy, to answer this one. P. Diddy said in an interview with Al Sharpton, "As a community we need to hold our vote... make them come for our vote... you have to bring something with it... I think we got a little bit short changed... I feel almost hurt that our issues are not addressed and we are such a big part of the voting block."

Other black celebrities such as Ice Cube, Kanye West, 50cent, and Shaquille O'neal spoke in support of Trump. You can pop to a video, "Hood For Trump," and see how adamant they want improvement for blacks and all people.

During a debate with Hillary Clinton, Trump spoke to the black plight, "The African-American community has been let down by our politicians."

On August 19, 2016 Trump looked into the camera at a Michigan rally and said, "Look how much African-American communities have suffered under Democratic control... I am asking for every African-American vote..." This was pivotal. This single act, and more like it, won Trump black votes.

Trump understood that voting *blindly*, for anyone, is a mistake. Specifically, that the tradition to vote democrat because you are black is a mindless vote. With this appeal, Trump received more votes from people of color than Mitt Romney, who campaigned against President Obama in 2012. And the black vote for Hillary was 5% less than it was for Obama in 2012.

Black power. It isn't what you think when the media saddles you with emotional haranguing, trying to dictate your response. Like any vote, it's in control of the people, and in the 2016 presidential election, black power was defined by what it did. It *changed.* And this is relevant only because blacks are part of the American people, like *all* people.

Democrats have long been trying to control the black electorate and the minority electorate by hook or crook, not in the interest of the American people or for love of humanity and America, but for power and the sake of being in power. To me, this is the highest form of cowardice, and highest crime.

Trump's frankness and direct appeal to the black voter, combined with their subsequent denial of habitual control, was echoed by everyday blacks across the country. High profile blacks like P. Diddy, Diamond and Silk, Sheriff David Clarke, Pastor Darrell Scott, and those interviewed in the "Hood For Trump" video (to name only a few) also voiced their support for Trump, or lamented Obama's failing to deliver on his promises to help black communities across America.

All this black power denied the democrats another blind scoop of the black vote, and formed a solid brick, in The Trump House.

THE BILLY BUSH TAPE!

Does every adult in America have a Billy Bush tape lurking somewhere in his past? I ask this because we are all human, and it's a great way to start a chapter. Right now, you are saying, well, what about me? Do I have a Billy Bush tape? Let's put aside for a moment who is "at fault" in all such Billy Bush tapes and let's ask, "Should we be looking out, or in? How important is "substance" when a man is considered for the Presidency? Four weeks before the election!

Personal events are important, but like everything, by degrees. After all, Trump didn't commit a crime here. And so begins my defense of Trumps comments, which I don't want to do just yet. Let me really begin, and I posit here... that indeed, the Billy Bush Tape *helped* Donald Trump win the Presidency. Why?

Let me explain by way of life experience and 11 months of pot smoking. Not by me! I swore off everything at age 27 and have never broken my promise. I take you to a personal friend whom I've known ever since early high school.

Let's call him Ekam for privacy reasons. Here's a description of Ekam. He didn't need to work after school, his family was set. He was an artist with a tall stack of books near his bedside, reading two or three at a time. He had talent, and the money underneath him gave him no uppity. He was cool and people liked him. He listened to you, casually but assertive in his opinion, when it was his turn.

Likewise, connected to this Ekam anecdote, when I toured Europe for 30 days on my bicycle, I left behind watch, cell phone, and all that, no credit cards, cash in pocket and took a penciled list of phone numbers in case I got in trouble. I slept in fields, I biked all day sunup to sundown. I saw a lot of Denmark, Germany, and France. If I had to describe each country with ONE WORD it goes like this: Denmark=clean. Germany=order. France=life. I describe Ekam in one word. Ekam=honest. Why?

Ekam had a sort of policy about his life - he smoked pot 11 months out of the year and took off January. He commented once, "To clean up." He absolutely stuck to this pattern for as long as I knew him. People knew who he was. There was nothing deceptive about his life, his movements, his needs or wants. However fortunate or unfortunate his circumstances were, this was the case. You could tell that people appreciated knowing what he was about.

People get jittery around uncertain characters, like Hillary. Now comes the Billy Bush tape, and personally when I saw the Billy Bush news (I remember exactly where, in the gym just out of the sauna, and of course there's a TV everywhere) I read the captioned words, "Grab her in the pussy."

I said, "It's over. Trump lost."

Guy next to me said, "Yup."

Seconds before that, I watched the Access Hollywood bus approach and right away I thought it would be a devastating story for Trump. Even without hearing any of the talk, there was something instantly ominous about that bus pulling up. In fact, I believe many Americans felt a story like this had been coming for weeks, and I was not surprised. (Later, we find it was part of a coordinated attack by the DNC.)

So there's the Billy Bush Tape, in all its "hideous and sexist" glory, according to our friendly news outlets. They did their best to tell you what you should think about it. But later, as the news began to sink in and the punch wore off, I was reminded of Ekam. Honesty. Private life. Deception. Lack of deception.

What was really going on here? Trump's comments do speak for themselves. I don't condone them, just like I don't condone doing hard drugs. But with these types of insights into peoples' lives, you get to see if someone is a deceptive criminal, has vices, or is just careless but not intentionally hurtful - you get to see that people aren't phony. When you identify with people who aren't trying to trick you, you feel as if you know who they are. You trust them, vice or not.

The CNN crew that made hay of The Bush Tape 24-hours a day. The network tried to drive a hysteria into women especially, to assist Hillary with the female vote. It caught traction with some women, as if they had been waiting for in and *wanted* to be hysterical about it, without giving credence to the total person and the facts at large.

Additional facts turned out to be a planned parade by the DNC of 12 women who formed an "inappropriate touching" bandwagon. Right on schedule, Americans didn't fall for it. They saw through the charade.

Maybe the American people said to themselves, "I know who Trump is now. At least he's honest. I know who this guy is and he's okay, he isn't trying to hurt me or take advantage of me." The prevailing FEELING is that the American people don't want phony hard-hitting politicians in office anymore. They want people who are real. Honest in who they are, not words.

The media tried to paint Hillary as The Most Qualified Person Ever To Run For President. That IS a joke. How dummy-down does the media want you to be? Only as much as they played the Billy Bush Tape over and over again. Ten-to-one negative coverage on Trump.

Trump, a man, partly with faults, a private life and boyish indiscretions (11 years ago) is like, well... like most every American, men and women.

The Billy Bush Tape surprisingly formed a brick of honesty, in The Trump House. And it came from an unlikely source, a secret tape about private life. Isn't it ironic that Hillary's secret emails revealed deception in public life?

LET'S SEE WHAT HAPPENS

I had difficulty titling this chapter. The other choices were:

"I'm all heart!"

"A man for our time"

"Willpower."

"Rudy."

Let's call it, "Let's see what happens." Although, you will see that all five titles apply to Trump's reasons for winning the 2016 Presidential Election.

During the months of watching Trump on TV and at his rallies, and later as I researched hundreds of videos, I found a motif in Donald very key to his personality, and probably a feature that is partly responsible for his success in life. He very often would wrap a conversation with, "Let's see what happens."

The more I noticed it, the more it grew on me. It was a funny thing, much like you would find a certain piece of music attractive, maybe like one from a larger piece of classical music. Like those chimes at in the Nutcracker Suite at Christmastime. They stand out, don't they?

You hear them right now, I bet.

I found myself using Donald's words. The first time was at the poker table. I said, "Let's see what happens," as a joke, while I was reaching out to call a big bet. I won. I even had the feeling I was going to win. It felt good to say it, and I wasn't being a smart ass, just kind of talking to myself.

I think open mindedness and positivity is a good philosophy for success. Maybe it goes like this: "Let's work hard. Let's prepare as much as we can. Let's be as accurate and honest as we can. Let's offer up quality as much as we can. Then let's then throw ourselves in the way of chance. Let's see what happens."

Similarly, it's not that hard to draw a comparison to Rudy. And God Bless Rudy Giuliani for being part of the Trump Team. For the Hillary supporters reading this, you have Rudy Giuliani to thank as well, who campaigned very hard for Trump.

Giuliani said many times, "Watch the video yourself, make up your own mind," concerning Hillary's disregard for human and the four Americans killed in Benghazi by her inattention and carelessness.

"What difference does it make?" she cried to Capital Hill.

Giuliani was not like the typical game piece in Stratego, a Sergeant, Captain, Bomb, or the dreaded Spy. Rudy was more like, Ulrich von Liechtenstein, Supreme Campaigner in Chief, Rudy Giuliani!

"When they come to save your life!" Rudy trembled, "They don't ask if you are black or white! They just come to save you!"

"USA! USA! USA!" The crowd chants.

Rudy Giuliani was a HUGE force during the campaign.

But the Rudy I had in mind when I think about Trump's outlook on success was Rudy Ruettiger. Who hasn't seen the movie, "Rudy"?

For those that haven't, real quick, Rudy Ruettiger was a real person, who's life was made famous by his ACTIONS, not by the movie. The movie was a byproduct of never giving up. Rudy was rejected three times by Notre Dame admissions. Eventually, he was accepted and earned a spot on the football team's practice squad. Rudy took it so seriously, that some of his teammates asked him to cool off. Despite that, after two years of taking beatings by the practice squad, he was asked to suit up for the final game of his senior year. Rudy's teammates urged their coach to put him in the game, and so, Rudy achieved his goal of playing football for Notre Dame, tackling the quarterback in the final seconds.

There is an important scene in the Ruettiger movie. After Ruettiger is rejected again, he visits a priest and asks him, "Have I done all that I can?"

Have I done all that I can? This sounds very much like Trump, who declared late in the election that he would do as many rallies as he could, including one in Michigan at midnight that spilled over into Election Day.

Trump said, "I don't ever want to look back and say that I didn't do all I could to win."

Trump doesn't give up. He works as hard as he can, and then says, "Let's see what happens."

He echoed the same powerful disposition many times in the closing days up until November 8. "I think we're going to win. I think we are going to do well. Let's see what happens."

Willpower - Donald Trump is 70 years old. He has displayed enviable energy with his three and four rallies per day, unending string of meetings and tweets, being part of his large family, giving interviews, and preparing for the new presidential cabinet and moving in the White House. The day

never ends for Trump. All his life, the will to
succeed, the will to learn from mistakes, the will to
understand what it means to connect with people.
He could easily have taken his money and spent it
on the beaches of Bali, forevermore. But here he is,
working to benefit all people. It takes an
uncommon will, and a big heart.

"No heart!" I think of "Jerry McGuire" often
when I think of Trump.

"I will tell you why you don't have your $10M,"
Jerry says to Rod Tidwell. "When you get on the
field, it's all about what you didn't get, who's to
blame, who under threw the pass, who's got the
contract you don't, who's not giving you your love.
And you know what, that is not what inspires
people. That is not what inspires people!"

Rod gets flustered. He ends up shouting at
Jerry, "I'm all heart!" and gets on the bus for the
next game. During a game not much later, Rod
gets his act together in a death defying moment.
Go watch the movie. It's another triumphant story
of "perseverance beating the odds." Like Trump.

People react positively to a struggle, if that
person is struggling for the right reason. For
wanting to do good for yourself, others, and for
breaking out into new territory. To improve.

Wayne Gretzky has said, "You miss 100% shots you don't take." In Gretzky's second season he broke legendary Bobby Orr's record for assists. In his third season he passed a record that stood for 35 years set by Maurice "Rocket" Richard, 50 goals in 50 games. Gretzky did it in 39 games.

Abraham Lincoln was a man for his time. There must be a match between current events and talent. How can one shine if there isn't a platform for him or her to do so? If Lincoln had been born perhaps two years earlier, chances are likely that the outcome of the War Between the States would have been different. If Eli Whitney had been born two years later, mass production might have offset schedules of industry in ways that we can only guess at measuring. Certainly, you can play the "cause and effect" game until you are blue in the face.

The point is - our times favor Trump. The right man, for the right job, at the right time. As controversy weaves in and out of our national conversation and news anchors scurry to find things to say, the American voter has decided. The people want change and we will see if the match of Trump to our country's needs, and the world's needs, is a match that proves fruitful, in The Trump House.

As Trump says, "Let's see what happens."

HOT SAUCE!

This event is so ridiculous it deserves its own chapter.

Hillary was a guest on the NYC radio show "The Breakfast Club" just before the New York primary. Sitting between a young black lady and two black men, Hillary was asked by the lady, "What's something that you always carry with you?"

Without missing a beat, Hillary replied, "Hot sauce."

People across the globe felt she was patronizing, out of touch, assuming, and insulting.

Check it at YouTube:
1. Hillary Clinton Hot Sauce Fail - #1 Way To Lose The Black Vote (or)
2. Bill Burr Reveals Hillary Clinton's Hypocrisy

Trump remarked, "It's so phony, pandering, so terrible."

Do you agree?

Sixty two million voters did.

That's it. End of chapter. Another brick, in The Trump House.

MEDIA MORONS!
FRONT AND CENTER! ON THE DOUBLE!

If ever there was a time to shoot an animal possessed with rabies, it's now. Rabies, and treason. This is disease the American media has, and that's the crime it has committed.

There's only one way to show you. Show you!

Donna Brazile, from CNN, was caught feeding the Hillary campaign insider information. Brazile sent the exact wording of a debate question on March 12, 2016 to Chairman of the DNC, John Podesta, cheating Bernie Sanders at a town hall debate. In her emails, Brazile wrote to the Clinton campaign, "Sometimes I receive the questions in advance," and "I'll send a few more." Brazile resigned from CNN shortly after.

Thirty eight top national reporters attended a dinner at DNC Chair John Podesta's house in April 2015.

CNBC anchor John Harwood sent an email advising the Clinton campaign how to deal with GOP candidates while gloating about how he provoked Donald Trump at a debate that he moderated.

Miley Cyrus calls Donald "disgusting" although Miley shakes a 2-foot dildo around on stage from her crotch, rubs it in her face, fingers herself to a preteen audience, lets fans touch her vagina, and rides 8-foot inflatable dildos in her underwear.

A woman waits 35 years to tell the world that Trump touched her inappropriately on a plane. The media runs the story night and day. Meanwhile, a video of Obama showing his erection to staffers on a plane goes virtually unreported.

(What is it with planes? Hillary, Trump, Obama, Loretta and Bill? Hillary falls walking onto a plane. Obama has a hard on. Bill is kicking it with Loretta. And my personal favorite: Trump's plane soars over a Ted Cruz rally in Cleveland while Cruz talks about Trump, who has just won the republican nomination.)

Media veteran Martha Raddatz, after repeatedly cutting off Trump's answers as a moderator during the second presidential debate, bashes Trump and cries on election night after Trump wins.

Hillary touched her face more times during the first presidential debate than when she had poison ivy as a kid. After each signal, Lester Holt tossed the conversation back to her so she could hit Trump with a prepared zinger.

While Hillary is being interviewed on her campaign airplane, a staffer instant messages a reporter three feet away. The reporter then asks Hillary the question she received.

A Politico reporter sent a full draft of a story to the DNC for their approval before submitting it to his editors.

The DNC leaked negative information on Bernie Sanders to The Wall Street Journal. Luis Miranda sent reporter Laura Meckler a letter from the Sanders campaign to the DNC whining about how "almost all of his nominees to the party's platform and rules committees" were rejected. He added, "You didn't get this from me."

The corruption and favoritism went on and on. It was becoming obvious that the media's reporting had essentially been Democrat propaganda, and people were losing interest in voting for Hillary. Saturdays and Sundays and even 3 a.m. were not spared. The media was unrelenting.

Every time good, working Americans came home from work and flipped on CNN, ABC, or basically any "news" channel, there was a banner racing across the bottom of the TV screen asserting that Trump was either a bigot, racist, misogynist, Islamophobe, xenophobe, or a cocktail of all these fears and inadequacies Americans are supposed to possess.

The media arm of the Hillary camp killed themselves trying to tie this "godawful" Trump behavior to YOU, into the American voters' minds, in order to s*hame you*, the voter, into not voting for Trump.

When democrat media saw no clear evidence that it was working, they devised a new attack - "The election is over, Trump can't win."

Congresswoman Nancy Pelosi declared multiple times, "Donald Trump is not going to be President of the United States. Take it to the bank. I guarantee it."

Obama - "I continue to believe that Mr. Trump will not be president."

Bob Beckel predicted, (after being booted from Fox) "The best-selling Halloween mask this October will be Donald Trump's face."

Ana Marie Cox, from the *highly esteemed* MTV news, declared on MSNBC, November 7, THE DAY BEFORE THE ELECTION, "The horror has ended and the monster (Trump) has been defeated. Now we can move on."

On election night, CNN reported democratic counties first, trying to influence voters in the west who saw votes piling up for Hillary (Florida) to stay home. Known republican counties in the panhandle and the on the Gulf side were reported last.

"Journalist" Jonathan Alter remarked on MSNBC after Trump won the election, "Decency lost last night."

Translation - 62M Americans aren't decent. If anyone displayed deplorable character, it might have been Hillary Clinton and the likes of Jonathan Alter.

MSNBC gets its own list:

Halle Jackson declares without statistics or evidence, "Trump will probably not win over some of these undecided voters," standing in front of Trump Tower, filling up airtime.

Lawrence O'Donnell mentioned Mitt Romney calling Trump a fraud more times in a day than he broke for commercial.

Mike Barnicle displayed an intellectually elitist arrogance after pinning Gary Johnson to his ignorance of the Syrian battleground, Aleppo.

Katy Tur. TOO MANY TO LIST! Here is one:

Trump caught Katy up short while she was trying to pin him to some negativity. "Try getting it out," said Trump. "Go ahead." She couldn't, she stammered. Trump continued, "I don't know if you're gonna put this on television, but you don't even know what you are talking about. Try getting it out." There was no substantive question.

Rachel Maddow and Lawrence O'Donnell repeatedly smiled and yummied up to each other and the cameras, fully expecting, as if the audience was so eager to participate in their joy of scandalizing Trump.

Morning Joe sidekick, Mika, repeated THREE TIMES, while staring dramatically into the camera, "Donald Trump, you have no idea what your words mean." Then she got sad, "I can't pretend to cover Donald Trump fairly. And put on a veil of objectivity. This is wrong. You have no idea what you are doing to this country." Then, a smug smile - she got through the prepared attack written by her producer, without screwing it up.

Mika sighs and exasperates in the background while Mike Barnicle explores a question that has no substance, "Across the great sweep of history, has their ever been a moment when the candidate of a major political party has opened the door to what Donald Trump SEEMS to have opened the door to?" The respondent filled up four minutes with gibberish, fishing around for an answer.

After Trump was elected, Rachel Maddow asked irresponsibly, instead of supporting her new president, "Is there a doomsday plan?"

I find myself getting angry at these people now as I write and relive this. One commentator called Trump "an empty vessel." Really? Read later about Trump's accomplishments already as President-Elect, more than Obama in the past four years.

Trump said it best at his rallies, "These thieves and crooks, the media, not all of it, but much of it. They are almost as crooked as Hillary, they may even be more crooked than Hillary because without the media, Hillary Clinton would be nothing... They control what you hear, what you don't hear.

"The media, they're not just against me, they're against all of you. Like Hillary Clinton, they look down on hard working people within our country. The media is condescending and even contemptuous of people who don't share certain elitist views.

"You don't read about that in The New York Times. The system is corrupt. The system is broken. The polls are phony. John Podesta rigged the polls by oversampling democrats, a voter suppression technique.

"The system is rigged, it's broken. And we're going to change it."

Voters agreed.

Those in the media who demanded that Donald had better accept the election results and honor the democratic process are now KILLING THEMSELVES. They must appear on TV every day and continue their jobs. How are they doing it? By doubling down and looking for more ways to attack Trump. The biased and unethical campaign for 2020 has already begun!

The bastion of bias, illustrated above, begs a question:

Since ALL their predictions, actually hopes in disguise, were wrong, do these reporters deserve to be listened to? Are they hypocrites?

These hypocrites, these campaigners for Hillary, CREATED the revolt against themselves.

The American people have built, instead of succumbing to manipulation, bricks: revolt against phony journalism, the passion for truth, fairness, and accuracy, in The Trump House.

UNAVOIDABLE PARRALELS

America is not an aggressor nation. We aren't trying to take over the world. For the last century, the U.S. has been a peacekeeping force to a large degree, defending democracy and aiding invaded countries. Not one of our 43 presidents turned out to be a dictator who murdered millions. The U.S. never started a global war, in fact, it ended one.

I state this straightaway to preemptively fend off the kook-jobs in the media who have treated Trump unfairly, because what I am about to write in this chapter deserves no spin whatever, into a conclusion about the heads of state who would now produce a similar result compared to history. The following comparisons concern primarily the populations at large and their similar feelings, in this case, motivations that created the groundswell for Trump, and the similar climate in Germany before and during WWII.

Adolf Hitler was hardly a "candidate." He actually lost the election of 1932, but only a year later was appointed chancellor by president Paul von Hindenburg, who canceled civil liberties which assured that Hitler could exercise dictatorial powers. Through intrigues, murder, and bribes,

Hitler had muscled his way into becoming Chancellor of Germany.

Trump, on the other hand, has been a candidate for the ages. Democracy has spoken in its highest voice by going the other way, shrugging off media bias and denying a corrupt establishment continuation.

Nevertheless, the people, in both cases, rallied around their candidates under similar circumstances. And what follows is *detail*. There have been throughout the last 50 years the inevitable comparisons of U.S. presidential candidates to past world leaders. Often these excitements don't get past "who bought who's paintings" or accusations such as, "those people in the crowd were waving their hands, like a Nazi salute!" It's rubbish.

What matters is the recognition of similar circumstances around *populations* when a voter swell is so large as to make world history. The unavoidable parallels during the elections in Germany 1932 and the United States 2016 are these:

Each candidate wrote a book. While in jail, Hitler dictated "Mein Kampf," to Rudolf Hess.

Trump co-wrote "The Are of the Deal" with Tony
Schwartz.

Each candidate had military training. Hitler was
a Corporal in the Bavarian Army. He was a runner,
a foot soldier who ran messages from trench to
trench. He was wounded once by an exploding
shell, then again in a British gas attack in 1918. He
received the Iron Cross. Trump attended The New
York Military Academy. He was made a Cadet
Captain, one of the highest honors for graduates,
and emerged as a star athlete and student leader,
graduating in 1964.

Each candidate juggled a league of generals
divided. The older and wizened German generals
of WWI were largely against Hitler as a statesman.
They thought "the little Corporal" didn't deserve
the title of chancellor, although other generals
were agreed in unifying the country around him.
Trump created controversy with American generals.
Eighty-eight signed a petition declaring he wasn't
fit to be president after Trump stated, "I know
more about ISIS than the generals." Other military
leaders lined up behind Trump and championed
him at his rallies, most notably, Lt. Gen. Michael
Flynn, who is a senior national security adviser to
Trump. Trump appointed Retired Marine General

James Mattis for Defense Secretary on December 1, 2016.

During each candidate's campaign, both countries were facing declining infrastructure. U.S. airports, roads and bridges are in decay. The Flint Michigan water system crisis is one example. The U.S. backlog of overdue maintenance is significant, and if not implemented could cost additional trillions in overhead and lost business. Germany faced even worse declining infrastructure of public buildings and private homes. Construction of new buildings, roads, bridges, and canals were so necessary, that they issued their own currency to stop the bleeding. Indeed, building the Autobahn helped revitalize the country.

Each candidate had massive rally turnout. In Germany it came to a hysteria. Very similar in that Trump turned the electorate map almost completely republican red, and while Hitler gained most of his followers by fear of persecution and dirty propaganda, Trump won votes by tearing down false propaganda that had been waged against him. This is a parallel, but an important difference.

Each candidate was closely involved with notable heads of law enforcement. Hitler was longtime friends with Police Captain, Ernst Röhm, (although later he had him executed.) Trump is a big advocate of law enforcement, and Sheriff David Clarke has become a close friend and supporter of Trump.

Each candidate argued against a principal contract that was debilitating his country. Hitler argued against the Versailles Treaty calling it "the greatest villainy of the century." Trump argued against NAFTA calling it "the worst deal in American history."

This next one deserves some careful handling. Each candidate rose in the climate of a scapegoat, or rather, one race is blamed for contributing to the downfall of the nation. In Germany, the Jews were used to convince the rest of the country to vote pro-Germany. In the U.S., the apprehension toward Muslims and refugees has been used to turn non-Muslims into votes.

To qualify, Jews were unfairly persecuted and murdered in Europe before and during the wars. They are now. But Jews didn't go on the attack and hijack a religion. Muslims that have chosen Radical Islam have committed crimes against America and the world. As I make the comparison of the two groups, as it relates to presidential elections, I am stressing the political factors here, the existence of one group to leverage against the main population. Not the direction of a crime. My feelings for all persecuted people and those that commit the crimes aren't available here. It's just a fact that in both elections, each presidential candidate had a group of people to rail against, trying to gain support from the larger group.

Each candidate faced an Establishment. Each could formally accuse the sitting government of corruption and self interest and back it up with facts.

Under corrupt governments, and when the rule of law is so visibly abused, the unrest in the population creates it's own symptoms. Why would the symptoms be wholly different from country to country? People to people? All the aforementioned circumstances and similarities could occur again in the future without much surprise. They are a relevant backdrop of voices, a long-cycle of political, planetary movement of people through the years. All countries stand on it. How people feel, why they feel, why they vote.

This global phenomena, the cycle, is a centuries-borne brick, in The Trump House.

Bruce Springsteen - The American Torch

Inevitably, there comes a changing of the guard. Let's get to it, and lift this icing off the cake.

Bruce Springsteen was in touch with the American people. He is no longer. Bruce Springsteen no longer carries the torch of the American struggle, despite his thoughtful lyrics from "Born In The USA."

You can pop to a video where Bruce is interviewed by NBC London in late October, 2016, just before the election. Bruce says, "Donald is going to lose," dipping his head with resigned confidence, "and he knows he is going to lose. Donald is a flagrant toxic narcissist. If he could only reflect..."

Look at this word "narcissist." In America, when such words are used in television and radio, they are usually twisted from their true meanings. Our perception today is that "narcissist" is "terrible," a selfish ritual of larceny between a man and himself. "Perfect" usually means "good." "Intelligent" has become synonymous with "smart."

These are dangerous and false definitions, often used to hammer the public with a media-born agenda, a media that hopes your are listening only half-way, or even subliminally. Just like Bruce Caboose is doing when he labels Donald a narcissist.

Bruce Springsteen might as well call Trump any name in the book, like a 'whathakapaedame," because Bruce doesn't know what he is talking about.

"The republic is under siege by a moron, basically," says Bruce. "The whole thing [Trump phenomenon] is tragic. Without overstating it, it's a tragedy for our democracy."

How can the republic be "under siege" in a free election? The PEOPLE have spoken. Why is Bruce taking a dictatorial stance? Observe, Bruce is not talking about Trump's agenda or his relations with the American people, people who are showing up by the thousands at his rallies. Bruce is surprisingly juvenile, calling Trump names and fictitiously characterizing that democracy is at stake when the very fact that "a person like Trump," has been elected is the DEFINITION OF DEMOCRACY ITSELF! Do these celebrities live in a magical hut somewhere, detached from civic life?

Trump was the ultimate underdog. When the underdog wins fairly, that again, is the definition of democracy. Even more so when the DNC and the

American media partnered to sabotage a candidate's chances. If any party deserves to be accused of being anti-democratic, it's the Democratic Party.

Trump won against odds so high, that when Trump announced he was running, the gambling site bodog.com put Trump at a 50-to-1 dog. That means you bet $1 to win $50, (minus the bodog fee). Those odds narrowed weekly as we approached election night on November 8, 2016.

On election night, Trump fluctuated between 3 and 4.5-to-1. At this point, however, and for the two months prior, the percentage of money bet on both Hillary and Trump favored Trump. Seventy-five percent of the money was laid on Trump to win. That's a leading statistic, just like Trump averaging 5,800 supporters at his rallies with less than 1000 showing up at Hillary rallies (including paid staffers).

As election night progressed, and "Bing!" Trump won North Carolina. "Bing!" Trump won Florida. "Bing!" Trump won Ohio, "Bing! Bing! Bing!" So did the betting odds change in Trump's direction.

The bodog.com betting structure went from (I personally watched this happen with my browser set at "refresh constant") bet Trump $1 to win $3 to absolutely stomping across all bets and settle at bet $1 and make NINE CENTS! The slate was taken down about a minute later and the election was over.

That's a gambling coup d'etat if there ever was one. It was a landslide, a voter repudiation, a smash of the establishment. DEMOCRACY EXEMPLIFIED.

And so, some of our biggest supporters of the American people, like the "all-knowing" Bruce Springsteen had no tolerance for believing in what the American people believe. He is not FAIR. HE doesn't listen. Let's not accuse Trump of narrow thought when America's darling Bruce Springsteen doesn't support the will of the American people.

How did Bruce become so loyal to a party, as to blind his eyes for equal treatment of Americans? If Bruce had a nagging desire to be a politician, he should have put down his guitar long ago and become a professor of law, a student of policy, and not just spout off emotionally and irresponsibly like so may others have done, such as: Miley Cyrus (fake crying by the way), Robert De Niro, Arnold Schwarzenegger, and Lee Daniels. Other celebrities have not packed their bags yet, although they promised to leave the country if Trump was elected:

Samuel L. Jackson, Bryan Cranston, Neve Cambell, Cher, Al Sharpton, and Barbara Streisand. Sean Hannity has offered any of these people a one-way ticket to a country of their choice with the stipulation that they promised never to come back.

How did these celebrities help Trump win? Right around April 2016 all this celebrity fervor was helping to draw the lines between those moneyed personalities living in never-never land and those who go to work everyday: farmers, mechanics, packers and pickers, food service workers, bankers, mortgage lenders, bus drivers, cashiers, road workers, and everyday people were becoming sick of the failed Obama administration and the "love" that the never-never land fairies blindly supported. (Scott Baio, John Voight, and other actors, to be fair, are Trump supporters.) But you get what I mean.

Bruce Springsteen was once described in a book about himself, "He is one of us, but better." I can't take away that honor from Bruce, and I don't want to, because maybe once it was true. But now I can't help but echo the same words to Donald Trump. Donald is one of us, even to those who voted against him, or didn't vote. He is here to help The People. That is Trump's mission.

Trump has a talent for connecting with the American people. He might be perfect and intelligent, or he might be imperfect and a doofus, but this doesn't matter in measuring success. What matters is Trump's accomplishments. Trump's detractors missed this entirely, or they chose to, focusing on style and not the result.

Using words precisely is the journalist's job. The same responsibility should also weigh on celebrities who speak out politically. Here's a great example of "accuracy fraud." Mark Cuban alleged that Donald is "lazy and doesn't do the work." Are celebrities high on their own wants? Such that when they want something to be the case, saying so makes it so? The detachment from reality by many celebrities is a serious issue for another book.

To be clear, we are not living on the holodeck on StarTrek. Mark Cuban was flat wrong and behaved irresponsibly on late night TV, for his own agenda. Do I need to cite any example that Donald is lazy? Let's not waste time but remind the Mark Cubans of the world that Trump is an action train with more energy that two Mark Cubans. Trump spoke at three or four rallies per day for weeks, at 70 years of age.

Throughout the campaign, media outlets, celebrities, so-called professional pundits, and pollsters used words so sloppily that they should have been stripped of their jobs. Many intentionally lied, betting that voters would be easily swayed because, "We have the microphone, and you are the dummies."

This is the moonshine they want you to drink. Propaganda, one-way, shinning in the night - "It must be true, because we reported it."

Now we know a large part of that news was false, because they invented it, such as the assertion that Trump and Putin conspired to win the election. How? Where are the facts?

The media has been lying and leaning on the truth so hard that even a powerful mind like Bruce Springsteen got caught in the apparatus. Can someone like Bruce really believe that Hillary is clean and squeaky-good for America? How does such a check-mate happen?

The answer is age-old, but made contemporary in Stephen King's, "Shawshank Redemption." The answer is: time and pressure.

Over time, our country has been indoctrinated into believing that we are the safe haven of the world, all the while letting our debt run up, jobs leave, and our standing in the world decay. How soon the world has forgotten that we SAVED the world from Nazi domination in WWII. Not alone, we did it with the allies. But without our American Spirit, will power, tanks guns and money, the world would be a very different place now. You wouldn't even be allowed to read this book, for The Ministry of Truth would have you locked in a room. You wouldn't have a front yard or a beer with your buddies. No right to speak your mind without fear of persecution at work, by your government, or even in your own house! That's how dehumanizing it can get.

America isn't perfect, but we have the best political system with the freedoms and rights of all people in mind, and the democrats will do any sort of deception and diluting of the electorate to stay in power, to crush what the Federalist Papers specifically set out to prevent.

The drug is lust for power, favors owed, favors being cashed, ambitious "civil servants" who see an easy and lucrative life in the method of lobbying and covering up the their selfish motive under the guise of duty and service. How corrupt would our country have become in this election, if not for the work of the few people in the media who are honest and gave Trump unbiased coverage? As well as those editorial hosts who support Trump. The short list is Sean Hannity, Laura Ingraham, Bill O'Reilly, Eric Boling, and Bill Cunningham. There are others, while ol' Bruce Springsteen didn't see the cuckold of the American people coming. The decades-long champion of the American people got hoodwinked.

Ninety-five percent of the media has been in the bag for Hillary, and the biggest media con job ever in America was floated over the people and it failed. It failed! At least in its electoral conclusion, yet, people like Bruce Springsteen chose party over people.

Has Bruce Springsteen sacrificed his belief in the American way of life, by way of telling everyone that, "The election is over." Bruce claimed he knew who would be President of the United States, before voting began! How shameful for such a provocative and talented American. Not everyone enjoys Springsteen's music, but it's not hard to recognize that he represented Americanism. The lyrics to "Born in the USA" are very telling about Bruce's concern and love of America, satirical though his words may be.

In fact, I was absolutely sick of hearing Springsteen on the radio when that album came out. I was working as a laborer that summer, every third song on the radio was Bruce. (In Wilmington, DE. Bruce lived close by in NJ of course.) I heard five different songs on five different stations simultaneously from "Born in the USA." I flipped the stations around just to see. You go into the deli and he's playing there. Get in the car, Bruce is on the radio again. It was worse than seeing Phil Collin's face all over the place when Phil went solo. Great drummer though.

A decade later, I would buy and come to believe "Born in the USA" was one of the best songwriting albums ever. Very sad to see Bruce being so intolerant, while he defines Trump as the same.

The American way of life has been in the lurch for years, and the corrupt Establishment, spearheaded by Hillary and her supporters, were almost successful in stealing its ideals from The Founding Fathers and from us all. Bruce Springsteen has handed over the American Torch to Donald Trump.

Bruce has succumbed to what John Adams and George Washington warned us early on, who understood the centrality of "checks and balances" so that neither Congress or the courts of the President might achieve "kingly" powers.

Washington, in his farewell address, was especially worried about party loyalty replacing loyalty to the nation itself. The majority of democrats either knowingly perpetrated this crime like a shark, or fell into it by design. Now we find out that even Bruce Springsteen isn't immune. And the American people felt the need for a big change.

The passing of the American Torch from Bruce Springsteen to Donald Trump is another brick, in The Trump House.

WHAT COULD TRUMP'S PRESIDENCY MEAN FOR ALL PEOPLE?

The best case scenario would be 1 2 3.

1. Countries dismantle, destroy and no longer build nuclear weapons.
2. ISIS and all terrorists are defeated. Brainwash-ideologies are replaced by a moral code that supports human life and the democratic system.
3. Poverty, hunger and despair are longer part of the human condition.
4. Hot sauce is outlawed to be carried in anyone's purse. (Alright, that's a joke. We need one, the world is a tough place!)

The world *is* a tough place. It's dangerous, brutal, unfair, and uncertain. Life can also be beautiful, inspirational, and rewarding. But we are looking to improve. The world is out of balance.

I don't need to tell you about the atrocities of the world, bad things happening to good people, the terrorist attacks, the crime wave, and the corruption. You see it on the news everyday.

But with hard work, determination and patriotism, in addition to the best case scenario 1 2 3, the following benefits to our country and the world can begin with The Trump House.

A. Racism is seen for what it is and vanquished. It's a business now, but has no place in the future. Race relations has been a fear that we grew up with. Fear is no longer taught, or learned through lack of communication. As mankind becomes more intelligent, and technology and communication advances, our ability to be help people is lifted. Our desire to no longer abuse "identity targets" diminishes. It's possible that this idea gets a major move in the right direction by example from Trump. If you look at this latest phenomena, 90% of the world believed Trump would lose. With 90% of the people acknowledging racism as prevalent in the world today, it could be true that great things happen for our people, that racism declines significantly. We again go the other direction from what people expect, and away from those who want racism to prevail because they profit from it. It's time.

B. Good foreign relations are unlocked. The habit of stonewalling acquired by Obama's is kicked. Trump talks on even ground with respected leaders around the world, governments and heads of business. All these leaders witnessed what the American media and corrupt politics tried to do to Trump, and they are now eager to work with Trump. They want respect and free trade like everyone, and they end up doing significant business with the United States that puts our GDP up 4 points in two years.

C. Health care companies compete for your dollar by raising quality of care and level of service. Everyone in the United States has full health care coverage.

D. Patriotism reaches a new high. People are proud of America, and the United States' democracy and way of life is the high standard that all countries strive to obtain.

E. For ALL people, even for people living where the United States isn't hardly in their thoughts, our new government becomes a better turn. Leading by example, Trump's straight talk appeals to the desires of hard working people and wins the day, his presidency accomplishes positive goal after goal, small and large. The world sees the improvement of our people flowing out into the world and casts off phonyism and no longer wastes time trying to undermine its own people.

America retained its democracy on November 8, 2016. The Trump House has been built, and the Trumps are moving in, and the American people are moving in with them. It is only logical and beneficial to look forward to positive change in our country and worldwide.

Trumpsters and non-Trump voters alike are primed to come together. It is no longer rained upon by the failed, "Change We Can Believe In" Kool-aid that Obama offered. Our highest office under Trump could be the epitome of "Change-In-Action." Not undelivered promises.

During the final days of writing this book, Trump has already negotiated with the Carrier Corporation and saved 800 jobs. He has also declared that a $4B price tag for a new Air Force One is too high. Trump is bringing 50,000 jobs to America thanks to negotiating a $50 billion investment from Japan's Soft Bank. Trump isn't even in office yet.

The Trumps aren't concerned about the drapes or the carpet. President-Elect Trump is already getting things done. He is setting up for a rigorous day-by-day action plan to restore America to peace and prosperity.

The Trump House has been built by many people and events:

Trump's tactical team at Trump Tower

Republican offices across the country

Trump supporters on Twitter and Facebook

The American people who listened with open minds

The revolt against the media

Desire to crush ISIS and confidence Trump will do it

A look into an honest private life

Hot sauce

Wikileaks

An examination of motives behind racism

A thirst to end racism

Hillary as her own enemy

Circumstances that matched talent with the times.

The White House will now be the House of The People - by the people, for the people.

In 2016, The American People built The Trump House in order to preserve The White House and democracy for our children.

God Bless America.